The Essential Buyer's Guide

PORSCHE
930 TURBO
& 911 (930) TURBO

Coupé, Targa, Cabriolet, classic & slant-nose models:
model years 1975 to 1989

Your marque expert:
Adrian Streather

T0386571

VELOCE
FINE AUTOMOTIVE BOOKS

The Essential Buyer's Guide Series

Alfa Romeo Alfasud (Metcalfe)
Alfa Romeo Alfetta: all saloon/sedan models 1972 to 1984 & coupé
  models 1974 to 1987 (Metcalfe)
Alfa Romeo Giulia GT Coupé (Booker)
Alfa Romeo Giulia Spider (Booker)
Audi TT (Davies)
Audi TT Mk2 2006 to 2014 (Durnan)
Austin-Healey Big Healeys (Trummel)
BMW E30 3 Series 1981 to 1994 (Hosier)
BMW X5 (Saunders)
BMW Z3 Roadster (Fishwick)
BMW Z4: E85 Roadster and E86 Coupé including M and Alpina 2003
  to 2009 (Smitheram)
Citroën 2CV (Paxton)
Citroën DS & ID (Heilig)
Cobra Replicas (Ayre)
Corvette C2 Sting Ray 1963-1967 (Falconer)
Datsun 240Z 1969 to 1973 (Newlyn)
DeLorean DMC-12 1981 to 1983 (Williams)
FIAT 124 Spider & Pininfarina Azzura Spider, (AS-DS) 1966 to 1985
  (Robertson)
Fiat 500 & 600 (Bobbitt)
Ford Capri (Paxton)
Ford Escort Mk1 & Mk2 (Williamson)
Ford Focus Mk1 RS & ST170, 1st Generation (Williamson)
Ford Model A – All Models 1927 to 1931 (Buckley)
Ford Model T – All models 1909 to 1927 (Barker)
Ford Mustang – First Generation 1964 to 1973 (Cook)
Ford Mustang – 3rd generation: 1979-1993; inc Mercury Capri:
  1979-1986 (Smith)
Ford Mustang – Fifth Generation (2005-2014) (Cook)
Ford RS Cosworth Sierra & Escort (Williamson)
Hillman Imp (Morgan)
Hinckley Triumph triples & fours 750, 900, 955, 1000, 1050, 1200 –
  1991-2009 (Henshaw)
Jaguar E-Type 3.8 & 4.2 litre (Crespin)
Jaguar E-type V12 5.3 litre (Crespin)
Jaguar Mark 1 & 2 (All models including Daimler 2.5-litre V8) 1955 to
  1969 (Thorley)
Jaguar New XK 2005-2014 (Thorley)
Jaguar S-Type – 1999 to 2007 (Thorley)
Jaguar X-Type – 2001 to 2009 (Thorley)
Jaguar XJ-S (Crespin)
Jaguar XJ6, XJ8 & XJR (Thorley)
Jaguar XK 120, 140 & 150 (Thorley)
Jaguar XK8 & XKR (1996-2005) (Thorley)
Jaguar/Daimler XJ 1994-2003 (Crespin)
Jaguar/Daimler XJ40 (Crespin)
Jaguar/Daimler XJ6, XJ12 & Sovereign (Crespin)
Lancia Delta HF 4WD & Integrale (Baker)
Land Rover Discovery Series 1 (1989-1998) (Taylor)
Land Rover Discovery Series 2 (1998-2004) (Taylor)
Land Rover Series I, II & IIA (Thurman)
Land Rover Series III (Thurman)
Lotus Elan, S1 to Sprint and Plus 2 to Plus 2S 130/5 1962 to 1974
  (Vale)
Lotus Europa, S1, S2, Twin-cam & Special 1966 to 1975 (Vale)
Lotus Seven replicas & Caterham 7: 1973-2013 (Hawkins)
Mazda MX-5 Miata (Mk1 1989-97 & Mk2 98-2001) (Crook)
Mazda MX-5 Miata (Mk3, 3.5 & 3.75 models, 2005-2015) (Wild)
Mazda RX-8 (Parish)
Mercedes-Benz 190: all 190 models (W201 series) 1982 to 1993
  (Parish)
Mercedes-Benz 280-560SL & SLC (Bass)
Mercedes-Benz G-Wagen (Greene)
Mercedes-Benz Pagoda 230SL, 250SL & 280SL roadsters & coupés
  (Bass)

Mercedes-Benz S-Class W126 Series (Zoporowski)
Mercedes-Benz S-Class Second Generation W116 Series (Parish)
Mercedes-Benz SL R129-series 1989 to 2001 (Parish)
Mercedes-Benz SLK (Bass)
Mercedes-Benz W123 (Parish)
Mercedes-Benz W124 – All models 1984-1997 (Zoporowski)
MG Midget & A-H Sprite (Horler)
MG TD, TF & TF1500 (Jones)
MGA 1955-1962 (Crosier)
MGB & MGB GT (Williams)
MGF & MG TF (Hawkins)
Mini (Paxton)
Morgan 4/4 (Benfield)
Morgan Plus 4 (Benfield)
Morgan Plus 8 (Benfield)
Morris Minor & 1000 (Newell)
New Mini (Collins)
Peugeot 205 GTI (Blackburn)
Porsche 356 (Johnson)
Porsche 911 (964) (Streather)
Porsche 911 (991) (Streather)
Porsche 911 (993) (Streather)
Porsche 911 (996) (Streather)
Porsche 911 (997) – Model years 2004 to 2009 (Streather)
Porsche 911 (997) – Second generation models 2009 to 2012
  (Streather)
Porsche 911 Carrera 3.2 (Streather)
Porsche 911SC (Streather)
Porsche 924 – All models 1976 to 1988 (Hodgkins)
Porsche 928 (Hemmings)
Porsche 930 Turbo & 911 (930) Turbo (Streather)
Porsche 944 (Higgins)
Porsche 981 Boxster & Cayman (Streather)
Porsche 986 Boxster (Streather)
Porsche 987 Boxster and Cayman 1st generation
  (2005-2009) (Streather)
Porsche 987 Boxster and Cayman 2nd generation (2009-2012)
  (Streather)
Range Rover – First Generation models 1970 to 1996 (Taylor)
Range Rover – Second Generation 1994-2001 (Taylor)
Range Rover – Third Generation L322 (2002-2012) (Taylor)
Reliant Scimitar GTE (Payne)
Rolls-Royce Silver Shadow & Bentley T-Series (Bobbitt)
Rover 2000, 2200 & 3500 (Marrocco)
Subaru Impreza (Hobbs)
Sunbeam Alpine (Barker)
Triumph Herald & Vitesse (Ayre)
Triumph Spitfire and GT6 (Ayre)
Triumph Stag (Mort)

Triumph TR2 & TR3   All models (including 3A & 3B) 1953 to 1962
  (Conners)

Triumph TR4/4A & TR5/250   All models 1961 to 1968 (Child &
  Battyll)
Triumph TR6 (Williams)
Triumph TR7 & TR8 (Williams)
TVR Chimaera and Griffith (Kitchen)
TVR S-series (Kitchen)
Volkswagen Bus (Copping)
Volkswagen Transporter T4 (1990-2003) (Copping/Cservenka)
VW Golf GTI (Copping)
VW Beetle (Copping)
Volvo 700/900 Series (Beavis)
Volvo P1800/1800S, E & ES 1961 to 1973 (Murray)

www.veloce.co.uk

First published in 2012, reprinted 2025 by Veloce, an imprint of David and Charles Limited.
Tel +44 (0)1305 260068 / e-mail info@veloce.co.uk / web www.veloce.co.uk.

ISBN: 9781845844219
Design and production by Veloce. Printed and bound by CPI Group (UK) Ltd, Croydon, CR0 4YY.

Introduction & thanks
– the purpose of this book

Warning! The Porsche 930 Turbo and its younger sister the 911 (930) Turbo models covered in this book require a very high level of driver skill and are not for the inexperienced driver.

Caution! Beware that Porsche 930 and 911 (930) Turbo are the most common cloned (copied) Porsche models after the 911RS, from model year 1973.

The information in this buyer's guide is arranged in user friendly chapters to allow prospective road legal 930 or 911 (930) Turbo purchasers to make informed decisions on whether to proceed or not with a purchase after viewing and test driving a specific car that takes their fancy.

The road legal version of Wolfgang Berger's 930 turbocharged racing car based on the 911 was produced to allow it to be homologated under Group 4 (Special GT) racing regulations. It was planned to build and sell 500 homologation examples of the new ground making turbocharged car. However, with the model year 1973 911RS, the still relatively new Porsche AG (changed from KG to AG in the big shake-up of 1972) totally underestimated the sales potential of its new car. By May 1976 (still model year 1975) the company had built and sold 1000 examples, and could have sold 1000 more. Total number of 930 and 911 (930) Turbo built cars had reached 23,163 when it went out of production at the end of model year 1989 (June 1990). The very last 911 (930) Turbo delivered was a slant-nose Cabriolet with over 450 customer specified interior options alone.

Historically, the 930 Turbo was responsible for introducing new word combinations into the Porsche driver's language: Turbo-lag, Widow Maker and Fun, but still hard to drive. All are forever associated with the 930 and 911 (930) Turbo model range. The time it takes for a single turbocharger to spool up to speed is

The Porsche 930 Turbo wide body Coupé was launched in model year 1975, originally as the FIA Group 4 homologation model. (Courtesy Tobias Aschbacher)

called turbo-lag, or waiting for something to happen. Widows are made when the turbo-lag is over and the additional power provided by the turbocharger is instantly unleashed to the rear wheels, causing an inexperienced and/or unsuspecting driver to lose control and crash. Finally, it's also renowned for its unique handling characteristics; a mixture of understeer one moment and massive oversteer the next.

New car imports of the 911 (930) Turbo model range were banned in some countries due to noncompliance with exhaust emissions regulations; USA model years 1980 to 1985 inclusive, and Switzerland from model years 1986 to 1989 inclusive.

The 930 Turbo introduced in model year 1975 was only available as a wide body Coupé with classic-nose design fitted with a 3-litre turbocharged engine and four-speed manual transmission. The 911 (930) Turbo introduced in model year 1978 was only available as a wide body Coupé with classic-nose, until model year 1982 when the optional slant-nose (Flachbau) was introduced. In model year 1987 Targa and Cabriolet body styles were introduced to the range with the classic or slant-noses. Until model year 1989 all turbocharged models, regardless of body style, were fitted with the 3.3-litre turbocharged engine and four-speed manual transmission. Adoption of an Alois Ruf design solution allowed a sufficiently

robust five-speed transmission (G50.50) to be offered in model year 1989.

Thanks
Special thanks to all credited photographic contributors mentioned in this book.

Contents

The Essential Buyer's Guide™ currency
At the time of publication a BG unit of currency "●" equals approximately
£1.00/US$1.26/Euro 1.20. Please adjust to suit current exchange rates.

– marriage guidance

Tall and short drivers

Left-hand drive 930 and 911 (930) Turbo models are more comfortable for tall drivers than the right-hand drive versions, due to the slightly twisted position of the right-hand drive pedal assembly.

Weight of controls

No genuine 930 or 911 (930) Turbo is fitted with power steering, so the wider the front tyres, the greater the workload required to steer it. It's extremely important that the correct front and rear wheel width and overall track widths are kept to within factory specifications for optimum handling. A vacuum servo (brake boost) system was not fitted to the 930 Turbo Coupé models. Brake boost was not introduced until model year 1978 with the re-branded 911 (930)Turbo Coupé model range. All 930 and 911 (930) Turbo four-speed manual transmissions (930.30/32/33/34/36) are fitted with a cable-operated clutch system, which is heavy on the left leg. The suitably robust G50.50 five–speed manual transmission – introduced in model year 1989, thanks to Alois Ruf – is fitted with a hydraulic clutch system that is slightly easier on the left leg, but not much.

Are you skilled and experienced enough to safely drive this Porsche model? And don't forget to check that it fits in the garage so that at least the driver's door can be opened wide enough to allow exit. (Courtesy Porsche AG archive)

Will it fit the garage?

Measure it and see, but don't forget the doors have to be opened in the garage to allow the driver to get out! Model specific dimensions are found in chapter 17.

Interior space

There's plenty of legroom in the front of a 930 or 911 (930) Turbo for driver and passenger, but the rear seats are essentially useless.

Luggage capacity

There is sufficient room in the back with both rear seat backs down to carry quite a lot of luggage, but keep it light; the entire turbocharged model range is sensitive to incorrect weight distribution over the axles. The front luggage compartment has sufficient room for a medium size soft-side bag, and this is where any heavy items should be carried.

Running costs

Porsche 930 and 911 (930) Turbo servicing costs are higher than other brands' because it's a 'Porsche' and it's getting on in years. Some parts are becoming impossible to find, and bespoke replacements may have to be manufactured. Old technology 3- and 3.3-litre turbocharged air-cooled engines burn oil as well as petrol. These engines generally do not use synthetic engine oil, meaning mineral (Dino) oil changes are far more frequent. Fuel economy is famously nonexistent, and it's even worse now because of modern blended low octane fuels – petrol isn't what it used to be.

Usability

The 930 and 911 (930) Turbo models are all unsuitable to be used as daily drivers. It's now, and really always was a track car and/or weekend warrior requiring tender loving care from the most experienced and skilled owner/driver. These high-powered machines with their legendary turbo-lag shouldn't really be driven in the wet, especially on twisting mountain roads, and should never be driven in wintry conditions.

Parts availability

As time goes by, parts availability for the 930 and 911 (930) Turbo model ranges is becoming an issue, especially for systems no longer supported by the manufacturer or vendor, such as the Bosch continuous fuel-injection system (CIS). Lack of availability is often used as the reason to replace original installations with modern equivalents.

Parts cost

Original Porsche parts that are available for the 930 and 911 (930) Turbo models are not cheap, and as already mentioned, in some areas owners are forced to purchase OEM (similar part, but without Porsche required design features) or aftermarket replacements. Sometimes the OEM and aftermarket replacements are cheaper, sometimes they're not. However, be aware that in some countries with regular mandatory roadworthiness inspections, checks are made on fitted part numbers, and if not original, they must have local certification approval or the car is defected.

Insurance
Check with your insurance company. A completely original 930 or 911 (930) Turbo, especially considering its well-known reputation within the industry, can be very expensive to fully insure. However, due to its age it qualifies in some nations for 'historic' or 'classic car' insurance, which can be significantly cheaper, but beware of restrictions. Also be aware that aftermarket modified versions may be far more difficult to insure. Check first, before committing to a purchase.

Investment potential
You will never make a profit out of a 930 or 911 (930) Turbo; it's just for fun. Any money sunk into the car will never be returned, and keep in mind that heavily modified versions may be hard to sell on at any price.

Foibles
Turbo-lag. Tendency to instantly switch from understeer to oversteer in the twisty bits. Clunky four-speed gearbox. Requires mineral-based engine oil. Limited availability of suitable size modern performance tyres.

Plus points
It's an iconic Porsche 911-based product. Excellent partner for a Mitsubishi MU-2 pilot.

Minus points
It's only safe in the hands of an experienced and above average skilled driver. It's getting old. Bad reputation in the insurance industry can be an issue in some nations. Lack of availability and cost of some parts.

Alternatives
Porsche 911 (964) Turbo, Audi Ur-Quattro, Chevrolet Corvette, Honda NSX and BMW 2002 Turbo.

2 Cost considerations
– affordable, or a money pit?

Service by an approved Porsche dealer
Intervals: 12,000m/20,000km (small) and 24,000m/40,000km (large)
Small service cost: from ●x399
Large service cost: from ●x698

Parts cost
3-litre type 930.50/51/52/53/54 engine top-end rebuild: from ●x4250
3-litre type 930.50/51/52/53/54 engine complete overhaul: from ●x6670
3.3-litre type 930.60/61/62/63/64/65/66 engine top-end rebuild: from ●x5250
3.3-litre type 930.60/61/62/63/64/65/66 engine complete overhaul: from ●x7670
Manual transmission rebuild: from ●x1600
Sachs clutch kit: ●x681 (including fitting from ●x1440)
Clutch cable: from ●x50
Zimmerman front and rear solid brake disc set including pads and sensors: ●x400
Air box assembly: from ●x260
Air filter: ●x24
Pair front windscreen wiper arm assemblies: ●x73
Pair front wiper blades: ●x29
Rear window wiper arm and blade: ●x127
Air-conditioning condenser blower fan assembly: ●x200
Rear blower fan assembly: ●x200
Sanden R134a engine-mounted air-conditioning compressor: ●x300
Ignition distributor assembly: ●x600
Distributor cap: ●x12
Set of sparkplug leads: from ●x175
Battery 80 amp/hr ●x133

Many 930 and 911 (930) Turbo enthusiasts do their own basic servicing at home. (Courtesy Tobias Aschbacher)

Structural work cost

LHD to RHD conversion: don't even consider it!
Complete body restoration: from ●x15,000
Full repaint (including preparation): from ●x3000
Full professional restoration from basket case: from ●x25,000

Manuals

Factory manual set: from ●x600
Original owner's manual: from ●x25

Parts that are easy to find

Battery
Windshield wiper arms and blades
Light bulbs
Alternator belt
Air filter

DIY home servicing is not difficult with the right equipment
...
(Courtesy Tobias Aschbacher)

Parts that are hard to find

CIS (Continuous Injection System) components
Exhaust emissions components (US and Japan)

Parts that are very expensive

This is a Porsche 911 so nothing is cheap, especially original parts, which are becoming increasingly difficult to find. Brake discs (rotors) and pad sets, clutch kits and exhaust systems are commonly replaced with aftermarket parts.

... but the older technology is getting harder to maintain.
(Courtesy Tobias Aschbacher)

3 Living with a 930/911 (930) Turbo

– will you get along together?

The 930 and 911 (930) Turbo models are not practical cars in any language. In fact, they're not even practical sports cars because of the high degree of skill required to drive them safely at high speed.

The original 930 Turbo was designed as a racing car and, whilst it's a 100 per cent thoroughbred vaccum servo sports car, it doesn't come with basic features taken for granted on modern cars, like brake boost and power-assisted steering: brake boost wasn't introduced until model year 1978 on the 3.3-litre 911 (930) Turbo, and power-assisted steering was never fitted.

Why do you want one of these? For the record, this was Martina Navratilova's Turbo. (Courtesy Porsche AG archive)

It's not correct to say that these cars were designed for driving on twisting mountain roads because they weren't. The 930 Turbo and its younger sisters were really only suitable for driving on high speed German autobahns, or on the race track with an experienced driver behind the wheel.

These cars are not suited for sitting in heavy city traffic crawling along for hours on end either. The engine is air- and oil-cooled, and the turbocharger is oil-cooled. The entire cooling system effectively relies on cool airflow at all times. Feeding the engine cooling system with hot static air from surrounding traffic is not ideal.

At the time of writing, the youngest 911 Turbo is twenty-three and the oldest thirty years-old. In its day, the 930 and 911 (930) Turbo models were not suitable daily drivers, and nothing has changed. These cars are event machines. Weekend warriors only to be carefully driven in decent weather.

The entire 930 and 911 (930) Turbo model

The race track is where the 930 Turbo truly excelled ... (Author's collection)

range epitomise the full Porsche 911 experience and of living life on the edge, but does such a car fit into your current lifestyle? Are you prepared to undergo an advanced driver's course? If not, don't buy this car. Do you have a family? The 930 and 911 (930) Turbo model range is designed for two consenting, crazy adults sitting up front with two tiny rear seats for luggage. The rear of these cars is no place for your children. Are you prepared to look after the car? As with any thoroughbred, living or inanimate, it needs lots of tender loving care. It's not the type of car that can be started and seconds later driven off, parked after a short drive, and the process started again.

What about exhaust noise? Is it going to impact on your family or your neighbours, or attract the attention of local law enforcement?

What about the money? You can afford to purchase a 930 or 911 (930) Turbo, but can you afford to own it? Are you prepared to pay the cost of ensuring it's always in peak condition?

Are you aware that many original Porsche parts are no longer available for this series and that aftermarket parts will have to be installed? Does fitting any aftermarket parts impact your nation's registration, insurance and roadworthiness inspection requirements? Are you aware that modern tyres are of significantly different technology to those originally fitted to the model range, and that the choice of suitable tyres is limited?

Purchasing any Porsche will impact your lifestyle, your family and your pocket, particularly the 930 Turbo or 911 (930) Turbo, being just that something special. Whilst the experience of living on the edge in such a brutal machine is worth every penny to many people, you must understand that this model range is more dangerous, frustrating and challenging than most. For some, such challenges just add to the experience, for others – especially owner's partners – it might become more daunting and dare it be said; dangerous!

… but with the right level of driving skill it can be safely driven at high speed on the road as well. (Courtesy Porsche AG archive)

4 Relative values
– which model for you?

Despite the fact that the 930 Turbo had the honour of being the first turbocharged sports car based on the 911 to be put into series production, it was only produced in one flavour: wide body Coupé with a 3-litre engine and four-speed transmission. When the 911 (930) Turbo was introduced in model year 1978, the only main differences were the new 3.3-litre turbocharged engine and an upgraded brake system, vacuum brake boost. The braking system was upgraded again in model year 1980 with the introduction of four-piston brake callipers fitted to the front and rear, along with perforated (drilled) brake discs (rotors). Apart from minor tweaks, the design of everything essentially remained the same until model year 1987 when the wide body Targa and

Model year 1975 3-litre 930 Turbo Coupé. (Courtesy Porsche AG archive)

Cabriolet body styles were added to the model range. The four-speed transmission remained, and the slant-nose option was made available for all body styles. In model year 1989, and thanks to Alois Ruf, the Getrag G50.50 five-speed transmission was installed across the model range.

Model year 1977 3-litre 930 Turbo Coupé with revised fixed rear spoiler (wing). (Courtesy Porsche AG archive)

However, all is not quite as it seems because the USA and Switzerland introduced bans on the 911 (930) Turbo model range. For potential Swiss buyers there are no real consequences from this action, but for potential buyers in the US there are. The US allows grey market imports, and whilst the factory-produced 911 (930) Turbo was banned in the US from model year 1980 to 1985 inclusive, large numbers of RoW market turbocharged Coupés were privately-purchased and modified (Federalised) for exhaust emissions and other US structural compliance requirements, and some were also converted from classic-nose to slant-nose. These

Model year 1978 3.3-litre 911 (930) Turbo Coupé with new 911SC in the background. (Courtesy Porsche AG archive)

Model year 1979 3.3-litre 911 (930) Turbo Coupé, and getting the ladies involved. (Courtesy Porsche AG archive)

One of the first slant-nose or Flachbau 911 (930) Turbo Coupés built for a customer. Headlight position is the key. Early 911 (930) Turbo slant-nose versions (and those fitted to the 911SC) had the headlights installed in the bumper. Pop-up headlights were added later. (Courtesy Porsche AG archive)

cars were converted in Europe and others in the US, but many of these 'grey market imports' had one thing in common; the conversions were to a poor standard, and resale values suffered as a consequence. Potential buyers must look out for unauthorised modifications, as well as wannabe Turbo conversions and look-a-likes.

Relative values between 930 and 911 (930) Turbo models are guidelines only, as any accurate comparison must include variables described in other chapters. Approximate model relative values are calculated using a datum point of 100% given to the most commonly available original 911 (930) Turbo; a model year 1987 Turbo Coupé with classic Porsche nose.

Model year 1986 911 (930) Turbo Coupé, which was allowed back into the USA. (Courtesy Porsche AG archive)

1975 to 1977 930 Turbo 3-litre Coupé **60%**
1978 to 1985 911 (930) Turbo 3.3-litre Coupé **75%**
1982 to 1985 911 (930) Turbo 3.3-litre Coupé slant-nose **80%**
1986 911 (930) Turbo 3.3-litre Coupé **90%**
1986 911 (930) Turbo 3.3-litre Coupé slant-nose **95%**
1987 911 (930) Turbo 3.3-litre Coupé **100%**
1987 911 (930) Turbo 3.3-litre Coupé slant-nose **110%**
1988 to 1989 911 (930) Turbo 3.3-litre Coupé **105%**
1988 to 1989 911 (930) Turbo 3.3-litre Coupé slant-nose **115%**
1987 to 1989 911 (930) Turbo 3.3-litre Targa **120%**
1987 to 1989 911 (930) Turbo 3.3-litre Targa slant-nose **140%**
1987 to 1989 911 (930) Turbo 3.3-litre Cabriolet **120%**
1987 to 1989 911 (930) Turbo 3.3-litre Cabriolet slant-nose **140%**

Note: Relative values have been calculated using reasonable sale prices. For grey market imports or federalised conversions of original RoW market models offered for sale in the USA subtract at least 25% from each relative value.

Model year 1987 911 (930) Turbo Targa. (Courtesy Porsche AG archive)

Model year 1987 911 (930) Turbo Cabriolet. (Courtesy Porsche AG archive)

Model year 1988 type 930S US market 911 (930) Turbo slant-nose. (Courtesy Brian Barber)

Model year 1989 911 (930) Turbo; the last of its kind. (Courtesy Porsche AG archive)

5 Before you view
– be well informed

The key to a successful purchase is research!
To avoid a wasted journey, be very clear about what questions you want to ask before you pick up the telephone. Some of these points might appear basic, but it's amazing how some of the most obvious things slip the mind. Also check car magazines for the current values of the model you're interested in – you should find price guides and even auction results.

Where is the car?
Is it going to be worth travelling to the next county/state or to another country? A locally advertised car, although it may not sound very interesting, can add to your knowledge for very little effort, so make a visit – it might even be in better condition than expected.

Dealer or private sale?
Establish early on if the car is being sold by its owner or by a trader. A private owner should have all the history, so don't be afraid to ask detailed questions. A dealer may have more limited knowledge of a car's history, but should have some documentation. A dealer may offer a warranty/guarantee (ask for a printed copy) and finance. Private sales = no warranty and all legal liability on the purchaser's shoulders.

Cost of collection and delivery
A dealer will be used to quoting for delivery using car transporters. A private owner may agree to meet you halfway, but only after you have seen the car at the vendor's address to validate the documents. Conversely, you could meet halfway and agree the sale but insist on meeting at the vendor's address for the handover.

View– when and where?
It's always preferable to view at the vendors home or business premises. In the case of a private sale, the car's documentation must tally with the vendor's name and address. Arrange to view only in daylight and avoid wet days; most cars look better in poor light or when wet.

Reason for sale?
Do make it one of the first questions. Why is the car being sold and how long has it been with the current owner? How many previous owners?

Left-hand drive to right-hand drive
Porsche manufactured its model range to comply with individual national requirements, creating specific left- and right-hand drive versions. The factory-produced right-hand drive (RHD) models were conversions of standard left-hand drive models. This is why for instance, no turbocharged models were delivered to UK, Australian or New Zealand Porsche dealerships with air-conditioning installed because there wasn't anywhere to put the evaporator assembly until the conversions were completed. However, some nations with right-hand drive regulations now allow local registration of left-hand drive (LHD) cars. Aftermarket conversions are very expensive and fraught with problems.

Condition (body/chassis/interior/mechanicals)

Ask for an honest appraisal of the car's condition. Be aware that in the 21st century a huge number of 930 and 911 (930) Turbo models on the market have been modified; some aesthetically and others more profoundly. There are also many clones/copies/fakes out there. Ask specifically about some of the check items described in chapters 7 and 9. A full systems check and test drive is mandatory.

All original specification?

A completely original 930 or 911 (930) Turbo model's intrinsic value is invariably higher than one with aftermarket modifications, but it's becoming difficult to find anything that's completely original.

Matching data/legal ownership

It's mandatory for any potential purchaser to ensure the 10-digit chassis number (model years 1975 to 1978), 10-digit Porsche VIN (model year 1980 only), or standard 17-digit International VIN format (model years 1981 to 1983), engine number and licence plate (if applicable) matches the official registration documentation? Is the owner's name and address recorded in the official registration documents?

For those countries that require roadworthiness inspections such as a MoT certificate in the UK or Fahrtzeugausweis in Germany and Switzerland, does the car have a document showing it complies? If an exhaust and/or noise emissions certificate is mandatory, does the car have one? Does the car carry a current road tax or equivalent type sticker or tag as required in numerous countries such as the UK and Germany? Does the vendor own the car outright? Money might be owed to a finance company or bank: the car could even be stolen. Many nations have Government or private organisations that will supply accurate and complete vehicle ownership data based on the car's licence plate number and/or VIN for a fee. These organisations can often also provide information related to the car's accident history such as: has the car previously been declared 'written-off' by an insurance company after an accident. In the UK the following organisations can supply vehicle data:

HPI	0113 222 2000	AA	0113 222 2012
DVLA	0300 790 6801	RAC	0808 164 1923

Unleaded fuel

Only model year 1986 to 1989 911 (930) Turbo fitted with exhaust emissions systems (oxygen sensor and catalytic converter) was designed to run on unleaded fuel only. Engines not fitted with exhaust emissions systems were designed to run on leaded fuel, which is no longer available in most nations. However, 3- and 3.3-litre turbocharged engines originally fitted to the 930 and 911 (930) Turbo range and designed to run on leaded fuel can use high octane unleaded fuel (98 RON), or octane boosters mixed with lower octane fuel, but be aware that engines will run slightly hotter and return lower fuel economy compared to the original figures. Beware of ethanol fuel mixes because the corn-based additive used in Europe and the USA absorbs water, which then becomes deposited throughout the fuel system. This can quickly lead to internal corrosion of major components within the fuel-injection system. If forced to use such fuels, never fill up from a pump with more than 10 per cent ethanol content.

Insurance

Check with your existing insurer before setting out, as your current policy or that of the vendor may not cover you to drive the car if you do purchase it. Do not drive uninsured cars, and if in doubt, always ask.

How you can pay

A cheque/check will take several days to clear and the seller may prefer to sell to a cash buyer. However, a banker's draft (a cheque issued by a bank) is as good as cash, but safer, so contact your own bank and become familiar with the formalities that are necessary to obtain one.

Buying at auction?

If the intention is to buy at auction see chapter 10 for further advice.

Professional vehicle check (mechanical examination)

There are often marque/model specialists that will undertake professional examination of a vehicle on your behalf. Owners' clubs will be able to put you in touch with such specialists. Local Porsche dealers may also offer similar services.

6 Inspection equipment
– these items will really help

Before you rush out of the door, gather together a few items that will help as you complete a more thorough inspection:

This book
Reading glasses (if you need them for close work)
Magnet (not powerful,a fridge magnet is ideal)
Torch (flashlight)
Probe (a small screwdriver works very well)
Overalls
Mirror on a stick
Digital camera
A friend,preferably a knowledgeable enthusiast

This book is designed to be your guide at every step, so take it along and use the check boxes in chapter 9 to help you assess each area of the car you're interested in. Don't be afraid to let the seller see you using it.

Take your reading glasses, if you need them to read documents and make close-up inspections. The author has to take his off for close-up work, so carry a glasses case if you have to do the same.

A magnet will help you check if the car is full of filler, or has fibreglass or carbon-fibre panels. Ask the seller's permission first before using a magnet. If permission is granted, use the magnet to sample bodywork areas all around the car, but be careful not to damage anything.

A torch with fresh batteries will be useful for peering into dim dark corners.

All Porsche models of this vintage eventually start to rust. A small screwdriver can be used – with care – as a probe, particularly in the wheelarches and on the underside. You should be able to check an area of severe corrosion with this, but be careful – if it's really bad, the screwdriver might go right through the metal! Again, always ask the seller's permission before probing their car.

Be prepared to get dirty. Take along a pair of overalls, if you have them.

Fixing a mirror at an angle on the end of a stick may seem odd, but you'll probably need it to check the condition of the underside of the car. It will also help you to peer into some of the important crevices.

Consider a camera as a mandatory piece of inspection equipment! If you don't have a digital camera, use your mobile phone. Take lots of pictures of all parts of the car whether they cause you concern or not. When you get home study them, and seek an expert's opinion. Sometimes photographs viewed in the quiet of your own home will reveal things you missed in the heat of the moment.

Ideally, have a friend or knowledgeable enthusiast accompany you throughout all the physical inspection stages. A second pair of eyes as well as opinion is always valuable, and it also provides a level of personal security.

Exterior

• Ensuring the 930 or 911 (930) Turbo is parked on level ground, begin the exterior inspection by looking for obvious signs of body damage, repairs, rust and obvious modification. Walk around it, randomly carefully placing the magnet on areas of the bodywork. If it sticks move on, if it doesn't, find out why. Specific areas to check are: metal panel below the windscreen (windshield), metal panel area below windows, door panels, jams and sill area, fenders (guards or wings), luggage compartment and engine lids.

Inspect the 930 Turbo parked on level ground. (Courtesy US Customs and Border Protection [CBP])

• All 930 and 911 (930) Turbo models were fitted with a fixed rear spoiler (wing). Two main types were used; the flat version fitted in model years 1975 and 1976, and the tea tray-type used from model year 1977 on. Non-standard fixed rear spoilers (wings) were also available via Porsche Exclusive for special customers. However, some owners have replaced the originals with a myriad of different aftermarket types of more modern design, including the bi-plane-type used in the 1990s.

Very smart-looking 930 or 911 (930) Turbo? Not even close! It's a model year 1983 grey market 911SC imported into the US now masquerading as a Turbo. (Author's collection)

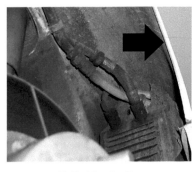

• External rust damage is easy to spot, as the paint will be bubbled and/or cracked, but a close inspection of the fender lips is required. Some owners have installed larger diameter and wider wheels, which initially rubbed on the bodywork. One fix for this problem is to roll (bend out of the way) the fender underside lips. If the work is done professionally, the paint will not be damaged, but if it's done, as in most cases, using items like a baseball bat, the paint cracks, and once the bare metal beneath is exposed to the environment rust will set in. The inspection for rolled fender

Rolled fender lip. (Courtesy Jim Williams)

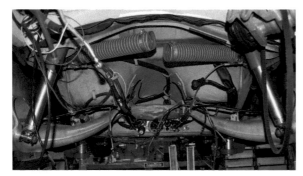
Modern rear shock absorbers. (Courtesy Tobias Aschbacher)

lips cannot be done at a distance. You must get up-close and personal using your eyes and hands. An untouched fender lip will be straight. A rolled fender lip is bent up into the wheel well. If the fenders are rolled, it suggests larger non-original wheels have been or are still fitted.

• Randomly measure the body panel gaps around the luggage compartment lid, engine lid and doors. If the gaps are even, it usually means the body is straight. Major inconsistencies in gaps indicate an accident or suspension issues. Regardless of findings, inspect all visible suspension components in the wheel wells. Ask the seller if the suspension is original. If it's not original, ask the seller how and where the work

Get up-close and personal and look at those gaps. (Courtesy Porsche AG archive)

was accomplished, and ask for all receipts related to the modification, including wheel alignment.

• Inspect for minor front or rear end collisions by inspecting bumper bars and the energy absorbing damper system on either side.

• Look for obvious signs of repainting, like different shades and overspray in areas such as forward of the doors and under the wheel wells. A poor repaint is immediate grounds to walk away. A good quality repaint should not deter from purchasing, but allow renegotiation of the price: down!

• Check around the headlights and front fog lights for stone chip damage and rust.

• Check the condition of the entire rear light lens assemblies, including the centre strip that contains the fog and reverse light assemblies. Look for trapped moisture inside the strip; if found, it indicates the seals have failed.

• Check the condition of all seals around the doors, windows and lids.

• Whilst inspecting the wheel wells, check the condition of brake discs (rotors), callipers and pads. Pad thickness must be greater than 2mm (0.08in) and the discs (rotors) must not be damaged. Look for grooves cut into the discs (rotors) and ensure as well as possible that they are even in thickness. Discs (rotors) that are below the minimum allowable width (thickness) will usually have what appears to be a protruding lip around the outer edge.

• If the 911 (930) Turbo is Cabriolet, ask the seller to raise the roof and inspect the

fabric. Faded and damaged fabric is very expensive to replace. Check the sealing and condition of the plastic rear window. Check the condition and alignment of the frame with the roof open and closed.
• If the 911 (930) Turbo is a Targa, ask for the removable roof section to be removed and inspect it and the mounting areas carefully.
• Look under the car for evidence of oil, transmission, brake fluid and water leaks (from windscreen [windshield] and headlight washer system).

Interior
• Do you like the interior colour(s) and materials used? Is it original? If these two questions can be answered positively, carry on with the inspection.
• Inspect all interior fittings and the seats for condition, ensuring none of the main or trim materials is cracked, torn, faded or missing.
• Is the steering wheel original (in some countries this can be an insurance issue)?
• Check for moisture in the front and rear carpets, especially if the body style is either a Targa or a Cabriolet, as these are known to leak badly if roof seals are damaged.

Don't neglect the interior colour and condition. (Courtesy Brian Barber)

• Run the electric windows down and back up to see if the glass picks up any moisture.
• Check the door pocket for moisture.
• With Cabriolet models, check the roof storage compartment for signs of wear, damage and water ingress.
• Lower the rear seat backs and check behind.
• Inspect the instruments for damage or fading.
• Check all electric seat functions and seat heating, if installed.
• Check that all interior switch assemblies operate correctly.

Compartments & mechanicals
• Open the luggage compartment and ensure the gas struts hold it up.
• Check the condition of the seal running around the compartment. Remove the carpet and inspect the paint, looking specifically for areas that have been repainted using flat textured finish instead of the original crinkle finish. Inspect all installed components – such as the brake system, fuel tank, mounting straps, screw heads, bolts, fuse and relay panel, air-conditioning system, valves and plumbing – for condition and any sign of corrosion.
• Remove the spare wheel and check around the fuel tank for water stains, rust and other signs of damage to the paintwork.
• Carry out a visual inspection around the battery, looking for rust and damage from acid spillage.
• Open up the tool kit and check that the contents are all present and not damaged or rusted.

... as is an engine bay inspection with intercooler fitted ... (Courtesy Brian Barber)

... and with it removed or not installed, as is the case with 3-litre turbocharged engines. (Courtesy Tobias Aschbacher)

• Check the wheel jack for operation and condition, and that all tools are original Porsche. Ensure the spare wheel and tyre assembly is of the collapsible type, that it is stored deflated, and that the electric air compressor required to inflate it is present.

• In the engine bay, ensure the gas struts hold the lid open. With the fixed rear spoiler (wing) fitted, the lid's weight is quite considerable, so strut failure is not uncommon.

Check for rub marks on the edges of the engine lid and on the bodywork. Look for signs of structural repair. Check the condition of the engine and as many components as can be seen, keeping in mind that the intercooler (installed from model year 1978 on) blocks the view from the top. Inspect for obvious signs of engine oil leakage.

Look for obvious engine modifications – labels with the letters K&N are a giveaway!

Is it genuine and legal?
If the owner claims the 911 (930) Turbo being inspected is a special edition – like the model year 1989 911 Turbo with Sport Equipment, which included a limited-slip differential fitted to the G50.50 transmission and an engine power enhancement kit taking its rated power output to 243Kw (330hp) – ask the owner to provide the paperwork that would have been delivered with the car to prove the claim. It's critically important, especially because of the buyer's premium asked for special editions, that authenticity is proven. Just because it looks right doesn't mean it's genuine. Also follow the creed 'show me the papers,' and never accept even the most plausible story without written evidence to support it. Once you've driven it away, it's too late.

Ask the seller for all documentation related to the car, including owner's manual, service record book, emission inspection reports, any import paperwork, roadworthiness inspection certificates and all repair receipts.

Check the service record book – is it the original or a replacement (duplicate)?

Under the luggage compartment lid, at the front near the locking latch, is a white label containing important information required to check authenticity of the car. Most important is the Vehicle Identification Number (VIN), which for this range of cars, became a little complicated. In model years 1975 to 1979 Porsche used a 10-digit chassis number system (eg 9305700124). In model year 1980 all Porsche cars were given a factory exclusive 10-digit VIN (eg 93A0070669), and from model year 1981 on all Porsche cars were given the 17-digit standard international VIN (eg WP0ZZZ93ZDS000011 [RoW]; WP0JA093ES050021 [Canada] and WP0JB093GS050331 [USA from model year 1986]).

From model year 1982 an identification (sticky) label was fitted to the underside of the luggage compartment lid, and an exact copy stuck into the service record book. This makes VIN and authenticity checks easier, but not infallible.

Ensure the paint code label data matches the car as well.

Ask the seller

There are some things that only the most experienced Porsche 911 expert is going to find during a 15 minute inspection. For the first-time buyer, it's much better to go armed with the important questions:

• Was this 930 or 911 (930) Turbo originally built for the market (country) it's being sold in? If it's the USA this question is critical, as the 911 (930) Turbo was banned from the country from model years 1980 to 1985 inclusive.

• If the Turbo is to end up in California, ask if it's approved for registration in CA. Until model year 1991 CA had its own unique requirements and was allocated Porsche country code CO3.

• Has this car been tracked or used in any form of motorsport events, including driver education courses and autocross?

• Is the mileage genuine?

• Has it lived its life inside a garage or exposed to the elements?

• Was it regularly driven in heavy traffic?

• Has the car been involved in an accident?

• Has this car's engine and/or transmission been repaired, modified or replaced?

• Have the rubber hoses and belts been replaced?

• Has the flywheel and clutch ever been replaced?

• Are there any known problems with any of the car's electrical systems?

• Are there any known problems with the exhaust emission system if installed?

Why all the questions? If you purchase any Porsche car with undeclared modifications and problems it can be very expensive and extremely frustrating to repair, and you may not be able to get it on the road or insured until you do.

Restoration of a basket case

There are quite a few 930 and 911 (930) Turbo basket cases around, but restoration is not an economic option unless the purchase price is very low and you are a masochist. Many turbocharged 911s have been resurrected from the grave by true Porsche enthusiasts, but such a project must always be approached as a labour of love, and expect to be driven totally crazy!

Get up-close and personal with the exterior … (Courtesy US Customs and Border Protection [CBP])

Wheel condition is important. (Courtesy Brian Barber)

Famous RUF CRT based on the 911 (930) Turbo, but there's only one like this. (Author's collection)

… and the interior. (Courtesy Porsche AG archive)

Are the wheels original and/or approved, and are the fenders rolled? (Courtesy Larry Hayes)

Yes, this non-standard fixed rear spoiler (wing) was factory fitted for Mansour Ojjeh (Courtesy Porsche AG archive)

Has it been used in hill climbing events? Ask! (Author's collection)

Is the engine type and serial number correct? (Courtesy Tobias Aschbacher)

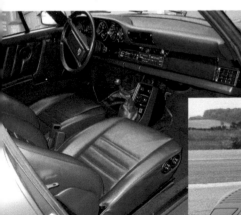

The most important question remains; is it genuine? In this case, yes it is, but in many cases it's not. 'Buyer beware,' and read this book. (Courtesy Porsche AG archive)

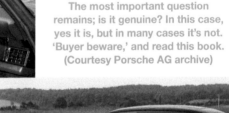

Check seat condition and that all seat adjustments work correctly. (Courtesy Brian Barber)

9 Serious evaluation
– 60 minutes for years of enjoyment

Score each section as follows: 4 = excellent; 3 = good; 2 = average; 1 = poor
The totting up procedure is detailed at the end of the chapter. Be realistic in your marking!

Porsche 10-digit chassis number identification system. (Author's collection)

Model years 1981 to 1989 17-digit international VIN system for US market. (Author's collection)

Identification label introduced in model year 1982 ... (Author's collection)

Any evaluation check must be realistic. Sole responsibility lies with the buyer to be vigilant and not cut corners during the next 60 minutes. Take it seriously, get it right and you will be able to make an informed decision on whether or not to purchase. Get it wrong and it could be your worst nightmare come true.

How does it look just sitting there?

The 930 and 911 (930) Turbo models are thoroughbred sports cars with a twist. These particular cars have no forgiveness in them, and if there are any defects that impact handling especially, they will bite their owners

... and it's stuck to the underside of the luggage compartment lid. A copy is stuck into the original service record book. (Author's' collection)

First impressions count. (Courtesy Brian Barber)

hard, given half the chance. Before starting the evaluation ensure the car is parked on level ground. Does it sit level? Are the tyres properly inflated? Are the tyres vertical or angled in at the top? Does it look original? Is it clean inside and out? Does it look smart or a little tired? Does it smell of fast food? What's your first impression? Rating is for your first impression.

What about the colour? (Author's collection)

Exterior and interior colour combination 4 3 2 1

One huge value killer can be unpopular exterior and interior colour combinations. Male hearts can be very practical on this subject and say; 'I can learn to live with it.' Rating is for yours and/or your partner's honest opinion.

Exterior paint 4 3 2 1

When inspecting a car's paintwork remember the old saying 'you can always replace the mechanicals, but you can never replace the body;' and the basic Porsche unibody is difficult to repair. In reality, there are two types of repairs carried out: sell on immediately repair and pass the problem to a new owner; or keep the car repair, but only if carried out by an experienced professional who won't cut corners. This is why inspection and assessment of the paintwork is critical, which is covered in depth in chapter 7, but if there are any doubts, take as much time as you like before making an assessment. Rust in is the mind, money and relationship killer. Rating is for condition.

Check closely for damage, no matter how slight. (Author's collection)

Body panel condition (including door bases) 4 3 2 1

A standard, unmodified 930 or 911 (930) Turbo sits lower than other standard road cars and is always in the firing line from debris kicked up off the road. If it's

Get up-close and personal with the bodywork. (Author's collection)

Rust is the mind-killer. (Author's collection)

completely clean, without any chips around the headlights, on the luggage compartment lid or outside mirrors, it indicates that the car hasn't been driven, or has recently been repaired and/or repainted.

Body panel damage, small dents and scrapes have to be assessed during inspection. Can any visible damage be repaired using the latest dent removal technology or is more costly repair work required?

It's also important to closely inspect the metalwork around the windscreen (windshield)

Headlights, trim and all seals must be closely inspected. (Courtesy Brian Barber)

and rear window, as rust bubbles in the metalwork indicates a serious and costly underlying problem. A close inspection of the fender lips will reveal if they have been rolled to accommodate larger wheels, and if it's not done properly (as many aren't) the lips will be damaged, the paint cracked, and rust will set in quickly.

Walk around with a ruler and measure the gaps between all moving panels and surrounding metalwork, which all should all be even. Compare one side with the other for irregularities as well.

Rating is for visible damage, fender condition and any rust bubbles in the paint.

Seals   4   3   2   1

Check the condition of all seals, especially those around the front and rear glass, doors, luggage compartment and engine lids and around the side indicator lights, if installed. Rating is for condition.

Exterior trim   4   3   2   1

Painted trim around the headlights often shows battle damage, and rusting clamp screws are an indication of potential problems. Rating is for condition.

Lights   4   3   2   1

Check all lights (including fog lights if installed) are functioning correctly. If it's a slant-nose with pop-up headlights, pay particular attention to the operation of the entire mechanism. For all headlight installations – classic,

Rear lights, centre strip and all seals must be closely inspected as well. (Courtesy Brian Barber)

bumper bar or pop-up – look for cracks in each of the lens assemblies. Ensure front headlight lenses are road legal for the nation it's being driven in. Some US market versions originally fitted with H5 sealed beam headlights have been modified and fitted with the European H4 headlights. Are the headlights properly adjusted? Will it pass a roadworthy inspection?

The rear brake lights and rear centre strip may be contaminated with moisture. Look closely for moisture, cracks and corrosion around the bulbs. Rating is for condition, originality, legality and moisture content.

Wipers   4   3   2   1

Check condition of the front and rear wiper arm (if installed). Assemblies can fade and rust. Check condition of the wiper blades. Rating is for overall condition.

Washers

4 3 2 1

Check the operation of the windscreen (windshield) and headlight (optional) washer system. The washer nozzles fade and crack, and can easily become blocked with car wax. Washer nozzles installed in the bumper bar are vulnerable to damage. Rating is for washer system operation and nozzle condition.

Inspect the rear wiper arm and blade, if installed. (Courtesy Porsche AG archive)

Cabriolet rag top

4 3 2 1

Cabriolet and Targa versions were officially added to the 911 (930) Turbo model range in model year 1987. There's some evidence that special construction Cabriolet and Targa examples were created for some customers much earlier, but it's highly unlikely one of these will come onto the market, and if it does it's going to be very expensive.

What lies under a Cabriolet roof's fabric? *Everything* has to be inspected. (Courtesy Porsche AG archive)

Check the Cabriolet roof in various positions. (Courtesy Porsche AG archive)

The Cabriolet roof system used in the turbocharged model range can be either mechanical or electrical, depending on option status, but regardless of the actuation system, a full inspection of the roof fabric, plastic rear window condition, electrical and mechanical systems is critical to enjoying the Porsche experience. Rag top fabric is difficult and expensive to replace, as is the plastic rear window. If mechanical parts of the frame system malfunction whilst the roof is being raised or lowered,

Don't forget to inspect the rag top cover when the roof is stowed. (Courtesy Porsche AG archive)

the fabric covering is often ripped to shreds, putting a serious dent in trying to enjoy the Porsche experience. Insist the seller operates the roof. Carry out a full and detailed inspection with it fully up and locked as well as fully down and stowed. Check the seals on the roof and structure. A bad roof is a deal breaker. Rating is for overall condition and operation.

Targa roof

Ask the seller to remove the folding roof panel and carry out a close inspection of its overall condition including its weather strips (seals) and mounting points. Check the car side seals and mounting points as well. Rating is for overall condition.

Check the condition and operation of the folding Targa roof assembly. (Courtesy Tom Uban)

Sunroof

If the car is fitted with the optional (M650) electric sunroof, insist the seller operates it using the primary electrical drive system. Pay close attention as it opens and then closes. The sunroof is operated by a single electric motor through a dual transmission and cable system. If one cable is worn or slack the roof panel will slid unevenly and may jam. There's also a hand crank back-up to open and close the roof manually in the event of loss of electrical power. With the roof panel fully open, inspect the roof water drains, seals and for any evidence of water ingress and rust. Also ensure the roof panel slides smoothly and evenly. Rating is for condition and operation.

Check condition and operation of the sunroof, if installed. (Author's collection)

Glass

Before carrying out a vehicle inspection find out what rules apply regarding glass damage. Is a single chip or

Windscreen (windshield) condition impacts safety and roadworthiness. (Author's collection)

Glass inspection also means door windows and outside mirrors, and don't forget to open and inspect the fuel cap cover and what lies beneath. (Courtesy Porsche AG archive)

Check interior sunroof areas (roof lining). (Courtesy Brian Barber)

crack sufficient to fail a roadworthiness inspection? Rating is for glass condition and how it impacts roadworthiness.

Suspension, wheel alignment & corner balancing

Walk around the car and look at the relationship between the wheels and vertical. If the wheel and tyre assemblies are seriously angled in at the top that means

It's critical to discover worn items like tie-rod ends during these inspections. (Author's collection)

that the current owner has a lot of camber dialled in or there's a suspension problem. Look at the wear across each tyre. Is it even? Is there more wear on the outside than inside or vice versa? Any turbocharged model with poor wheel alignment will cause tyres to wear unevenly, creating a potentially dangerous situation; a turbocharged Porsche needs all the grip it can get. Check for aftermarket suspension modifications, usually indicated by the colour of the front struts, shock absorbers and springs. If in doubt, ask the seller. Corner balancing (weight distribution over each wheel) is accomplished using weights in the bumper bars. If the car is totally original, it can be assumed the weights are still in place, but what if the bumper bars have been replaced? Bad weight distribution affects handling and tyre wear. Unfortunately, handling can only be checked on a spirited test drive, but look for clues during the static inspection. Rating is for overall suspension condition, evidence of aftermarket modifications and findings that may affect the wheel alignment and/or corner balancing.

It's hard to see much in the wheel wells with front ... (Author's collection)

... and rear wheels still fitted and the car standing on the ground, but it looks a bit grim. Those tyres are a little suspect as well! (Author's collection)

Wheels   4️⃣ 3️⃣ 2️⃣ 1️⃣

The 930 Turbo model range was originally fitted with 7Jx15 front and 8Jx15 rear wheels. In model year 1977 the wheel size was changed to 7Jyx16 front and 8Jx16 rear.

The 911 (930) Turbo model range began using the same wheel sizes as its predecessor, but eventually a 9Jx16 rear wheel was added to the mix. In the 21st century it would be very rare to find a 930 Turbo from model years 1975 and 1976 still fitted with 15in diameter wheels, as suitable tyres are almost impossible to find.

Check the fitted wheels are correct for the model range by checking the owner's manual. In some countries non-standard wheels require special approval. Wheel condition is also important. Corrosion can cause the wheel to crack and fail. Rating is for wheel originality,

Factory installed wheels? Yes. (Courtesy Porsche AG archive)

evidence of rolled fenders and/or wheel rub and condition.

4 3 2 1

Wheel wells

Wheel wells can reveal a multitude of sins. Rolled fender lips to accommodate larger wheels have been mentioned a few times. The right front wheel well houses the auxiliary oil cooler; it's not uncommon to find the basic and ineffective trombone or finned pipe versions replaced by radiator core type oil coolers with or without cooling fan. Porsche Exclusive and some owners privately

Original 1970s RoW market type oil cooler installed in the right front wheel well … (Courtesy Lee and Jay Heppe)

… and they didn't make oil coolers with fans in model year 1979! (Author's collection)

The oil tank is located in the right rear wheel well behind the wheel. (Courtesy Tobias Aschbacher)

Porsche Exclusive-installed front centre oil cooler radiator assembly. (Courtesy Porsche AG archive)

Windscreen (windshield) washer water tank is located in the left front wheel well. (Courtesy Andy Leadbetter)

The oil filter can only be accessed from underneath. (Courtesy Steve Shanks)

This halfshaft and CV joint is not in good condition, and may need replacing. (Courtesy Steve Shanks)

installed an additional centre-mounted oil cooler originally designed for the 930/934/935 racing cars. If in doubt, ask the seller. The rear section of the right rear wheel well contains the external oil tank, and the forward section contains the auxiliary oil cooler thermostat. Inspect all these items in the oil cooling circuit very closely. Rating is for condition, and for any evidence of oil leaks.

Wheel bearings & halfshafts

Porsche 911 wheel bearings are almost bulletproof and rarely fail; if anything screams like a banshee whilst driving, it's more likely to be the CV joint of the halfshaft, which connects the transaxle transmission to each rear wheels. To check the wheel bearing remove the wheel centre cap and use a torch to inspect for evidence of metal filings and overheating. A failed wheel bearing will get so hot that it will blue the cotter pin, burn the lubricating grease within the bearing and deposit soot around the wheel bearing housing. If metal debris or evidence of overheating is discovered, jack the affected wheel off the ground and rotate it. If grinding, scrapping noises are heard, it's likely either the wheel bearing and/or the halfshaft CV joint has failed.

The test drive will reveal any rotating part with failed bearing surfaces because, as mentioned above, it will scream like a banshee. Locating the source of the noise however, will require a thorough inspection. Rating is for condition of the wheel bearing and if further, more detailed inspection is warranted.

Tyre condition & suitability

Who owns a thoroughbred sports car capable of delivering large amounts of horsepower instantly to the rear wheels and installs cheap tyres or mixes and matches brands and treads in order to save money? Answer: Many owners do, and it's extremely dangerous. The four black round bits of rubber wrapped around the wheels are the only things separating the car from the road, and in the case of the turbocharged model range, the only things holding the car on the road when the power comes on. Why spend a large amount of money purchasing a precision high-performance, and in this case iconic and precious sports car and put yourself and everyone else at risk by fitting cheap, unsuitable tyres? Remember, the engine is installed in the rear, so where is the greatest load or weight going to be

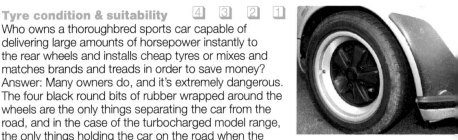

See chapter 17 for the Porsche tyres table. Tyre condition is a safety issue. (Author's collection)

and where is the power transmitted into the ground? Answer: Over the rear and through the rear tyres. Which tyres require the greater strength (load factor), front or rear? Answer: The rear. So why install cheap tyres designed for a car with its engine installed in the front? It's true that the original tyres and sizes designed for the early models in particular are no longer available, but there's a list of modern tyres tested by Porsche AG in the summer of 2008 (see chapter 17). Check the tyres for: condition, age, same brand, same tread pattern, correct size for the installed wheels. Rating is for tyre condition (bubbles and cracks), wear (even/ uneven), age (more than six years old) and suitability for this iconic sports car.

Brake booster (911 [930] Turbo only), fluid reservoir and master cylinder. (Courtesy Brian Barber)

Dealer-installed air-conditioning evaporator for RHD 911. (Courtesy Andy Leadbetter)

Steering system

All turbocharged 930 and 911 (930) models are fitted with a non-power-assisted steering system. The only checks that can be carried out are for wear: the steering wheel can be turned left and right without moving the wheels, does not sit centred whilst driving and/or the car tracks right or left whilst moving. Worn steering

Brake callipers are very hard to inspect properly through standard wheels. (Courtesy Brian Barber)

911 (930) Turbo brake calliper. (Courtesy Tobias Aschbacher)

arms and tie-rod ends (ball joints) are not uncommon with older cars. Rating is for condition and wear.

Brake callipers, pads & boost system

Up to and including model year 1979 all the turbocharged 930 and 911 (930) models were fitted with front (A-type) and rear (M-type) cast iron 2-piston brake callipers. From model year 1980 all turbocharged models were fitted with a set of aluminium alloy 4-piston front and rear brake callipers. These brake callipers remained the standard top of the line system available form Porsche AG until well into the 1990s. There should be no reason that they've been changed, but as always, if in doubt ask the seller.

Brake pad minimum thickness is 2mm. (Courtesy Gary Cuozzo)

Check the brake pads are more than 2mm (0.08in) thick or they'll need replacing. The brake boost system (from model year 1978) and fluid reservoir is installed in the luggage compartment, and can be inspected as part of this section's inspection regime. Rating is for calliper originality and condition, as well thickness of brake pads.

Brake discs (rotors)
Prior to model year 1980 turbocharged models were delivered with ventilated solid front and rear brake discs (rotors). From model year 1980 on all turbocharged models were delivered with ventilated and perforated (drilled holes) front and rear brake discs (rotors). It is normal in the 21st century to only find drilled or slotted brake discs (rotors) fitted. Check brake disc (rotor) wear, looking for grooves cut into the disc (rotor). Consideration has to be given to overall brake disc (rotor) thickness, which, during such an evaluation, is hard to check. Look at each disc (rotor) carefully. Is there a lip or edge cut around the outer circumference? Such a lip indicates that the brake pads have worn away both faces of the disc (rotor), and at the next service all will have to be replaced. Rating is for brake disc (rotor) condition.

Vented and perforated (drilled) brake discs (rotors) introduced for model year 1980. (Courtesy Gary Cuozzo)

Hand (emergency or park) brake
The hand (emergency or park) brake must be tested to ensure it holds the car under all circumstances. Rating is for the hand (emergency or park) brake holding ability.

Rear spoiler
All turbocharged models were delivered with a fixed rear spoiler of the flat or tea tray or whale tail types. Some special customer models were built with a type 935 rear spoiler (wing) installed. However, such factory installations are rare, so if the fitted type doesn't look original, ask the seller. During inspection pay particular attention to the condition of the rear spoiler's (wing's) rubber components, as these deteriorate and repair costs can be high. Rating is for condition.

**Engine bay
top inspection**

One of two hand (emergency/park) brake actuator assemblies behind each rear wheel. (Courtesy Keith Sheu)

Check the car's documentation against what engine size is fitted. All original engine types are prefixed with 930. The 930 model range was fitted with 3-litre single turbocharged engines without an intercooler. The 911 (930) model range was fitted with 3.3-litre single turbocharged engines with an intercooler. All 930 turbocharged

3-litre turbocharged engine without intercooler. (Author's collection)

3.3-litre turbocharged engine. (Courtesy Brian Barber)

engines used the Bosch K-tronic CIS (Continuous Injection System) fuel-injection system. Once the engine has been verified as original, the first check in the engine bay is to smell for fuel. Ask the seller when the rubber hoses were last replaced; pin holes will develop in fuel and vacuum lines once the rubber starts to degrade. Check the engine-driven alternator, secondary air injection pump and air-conditioning compressor (if installed) drive belts. Ask the seller when these were last replaced. Look around for corrosion in the crankcase and check the condition of all visible components, remembering that the intercooler will impede access and view. If any alarm bells are ringing, ask the seller. Inspecting the underside of the engine will be covered later. Rate the engine bay top inspection on condition of all visible components, originality, all visible metalwork, and engine bay cleanliness.

A condenser-mixer is installed in the top of the engine bay lid – inspect. (Courtesy Brian Barber)

Fuel cap cover & luggage compartment

Open the fuel cap cover located in the left side fender (guard/wing) using the dash-mounted cable release mechanism. Check the condition of the fuel cap cover, and ensure the fuel type label is installed on the underside of the lid. Check the condition of the fuel cap and the windscreen (windshield) washer filling point. Close the fuel cap cover and ensure it locks in place.

Open the luggage compartment lid using the installed cable release mechanism. Release the lid from the safety lock and lift it up to its fully open position, ensuring

Luggage compartment with carpet, and the tool roll laid out for inspection. (Courtesy Brian Barber)

Luggage compartment with carpet removed, and all is exposed. (Courtesy Brian Barber)

the gas struts hold it up. After inspecting the carpet condition, remove the carpet to expose what lies beneath. Check the fuel tank, brake master cylinder, fluid reservoir and vacuum brake booster (if installed) assembly (location dependent on left- or right-hand drive) for condition and evidence of fluid leaks. Check labels on the battery to identify its capacity and age. Next, inspect the collapsible spare wheel fitted into the fuel tank. Remove the spare wheel, inspect it and then check the condition of the fuel tank where it mounts. Check that there's an air compressor in the car because without it the spare is useless. Ensure the wheel jack and associated accessories are installed, along with a

Luggage compartment relay and fuse panel with cover removed. (Courtesy Porsche AG archive)

reflective triangle, tow hook and tool roll. Open up the tool roll and check that all the tools are accounted for and condition. Sustained water ingress will cause the tools to rust. Rating is for carpet condition, installed component condition, compartment structure condition (including rust, water staining, brake fluid damage, battery acid damage and any evidence of paint overspray and/or crash repairs), condition of the spare wheel, all accessories, tools and emergency equipment.

Note: Do not reinstall the carpet; it needs to be removed for some of the checks that follow.

Battery charging rate

With the engine running at idle, connect a digital multi-meter across the battery terminals. The voltage displayed must be between 13.8 and 14.2V DC. To check

battery condition, turn the engine off and measure the voltage between the terminals again; it should be between 12.4 and 12.6V DC.

Rating is based on voltage measurements in both tests. For example: 13.8V DC and 12.6V DC = 4. More than 14.2V DC and less than 12.4V DC = 1.

Relay & fuse panel   ④ ③ ② ①

With the carpet removed, locate the relay and fuse panel in the luggage compartment. Remove the cover and compare the relay and fuse contents with those shown in the owner's manual. Also check for corrosion on and around all electrical connections. Rating is for condition of all relays and fuses and any evidence of corrosion. **Note:** Now reinstall the carpet.

Checking the battery is easy, and this one failed: voltage too low. (Courtesy Larry Turner)

Interior water ingress check   ④ ③ ② ①

Open the doors and check along the bottom of each door for water. Run the electric windows down and up to see if the window picks up any moisture. Open each door storage compartment checking for obvious signs of dampness or water damaged contents. Dab a tissue around any suspect areas inside the car, including the carpets, to see if it picks up any moisture. Expect to find moisture damage in Targa and Cabriolet models that live in wet environments. Rating is for how much moisture is discovered.

Interior   ④ ③ ② ①

The interior inspection is all about originality and condition of installed seats, seat belts, dash, carpet, mats and trim. Inspect for rips, tears, staining, mould, repairs and frayed seat belts. Obvious modifications to either inspect for or ask the seller about include racing seats, racing harnesses and stereo system replacement. Check that all the interior lights function when the doors are opened (on) and closed (off). Check the condition of the roof liner. If a sunroof is fitted, the roof liner will have a zip installed for access to the roof drive mechanism. Check its condition and operation. Check all mechanical seat functions in accordance with the owner's manual. Check that the rear seat backs can be lowered and locked back into placed when raised. Check the condition of the rear parcel shelf cover.

Rating is for overall condition, operation of mechanical seat functions, interior lighting operation and discovered modifications.

Steering wheel and horn   ④ ③ ② ①

Inspect the steering wheel for condition. Check horn operation. Rating is for steering wheel condition and horn operation.

Interior: condition, colour and originality, and yes, this is from Porsche Exclusive.
(Courtesy Porsche AG archive)

Steering column control stalks

Check all installed steering wheel stalk functions. Turn on the headlights and check the high and low beam. Leave the head lights on and check all installed wiper and washer systems. Rating is for condition of each stalk and all systems operation.

Instruments

Have instrument dials been replaced with white or yellow aftermarket versions? Are the instruments vertical or have they been twisted? If twisted this is a potential clue that the car may have spent some time on the race track. Check each instrument for originality and condition, including the bezel (has a screwdriver been used to pry the instrument out?). Rating is for instrument originality and condition.

Warning lights

Consult the owner's manual warning light pages. Warning lights are model and version specific. Ensure what's required is fitted and working. Rating is for originality and functionality of fitted warning lights: whilst the car is powered, but engine not running; with engine running, but not moving; and during the test drive.

The next stage is to put the car onto a lifter or over a maintenance pit and carry out some basic inspections from underneath.

Structural component inspection

Using a torch (flashlight), mirror and probe, inspect the entire underside structure and structural fittings for evidence of rust, crash damage and fresh welding. Ensure

the underside panels are fitted and in good condition. Rating is for evidence of rust, damage, repair and overall condition.

4 3 2 1

Exhaust system
Ask the seller if any exhaust modifications have been carried out. There isn't a rear engine cover fitted to the 930 and 911 (930) turbocharged model range, so most of the engine and systems can be seen from underneath. Don't forget that US market versions from model year 1986 on are fitted with a catalytic converter and an oxygen sensor. Japanese versions are fitted with a catalytic converter, oxygen sensor and exhaust

temperature sensor. It's not uncommon in the USA, in states that do not have mandatory exhaust emission inspections, to find that the catalytic converter has been removed and replaced with a bypass pipe. Unfortunately, this may become a serious problem for any new owner if the car is to cross state or international borders. Check the entire exhaust system, including the heat exchangers for rust damage and holes. Rating is for originality and condition.

Oil leaks

One of the best oil leak checks that can be carried out is done after the test drive. Park the car on level ground and slide some butcher's paper under the engine and behind the front right wheel to check the oil cooler system for leaks. Leave it there for 30 to 60 minutes, then pull out the paper and check how much oil has dripped onto it. Major oil leaks should be evident during the underside inspection. Rating is for any detected oil leaks during the static inspection and after the test drive.

Transmission fluid leaks

Ensure a sufficient amount of paper is placed under the entire transmission to catch any fluid drips. Rating is for any detected leaks.

Water leaks

Water leaking onto the ground is only normal if the car is fitted with air-conditioning. The only other water source is the windscreen (windshield) washer tank, which shouldn't leak. Rating is for any detected leaks.

Test drive

This is mandatory. During the test drive every system must be tested, including the air-conditioning, heating, sound, etc. Everything with a button must be switched on and tested. The test drive rating must reflect the correct function of every system, handling, braking efficiency, acceleration and gear changing and the intensity of the smile on your face.

Playing hard ball

This might be the result of playing hardball with the seller. (Courtesy Tobias Aschbacher)

The basic type 930 turbocharged engine is bulletproof, but even so, most originally-installed engines have very high operating times in the 21st century. Therefore, a top end rebuild or full overhaul is likely to be required in the near future. However, some buyers demand engine leak down and compression checks be carried out to check the internal condition of the engine. Such checks require invasive surgery, and many sellers refuse. It is true there's no other way of determining engine internal condition – apart from obvious pointers like it's blowing smoke or is seriously down on power, which can be hard to determine until turbo-lag has been overcome – but use some common sense and understand that very few people know how to do leak down checks properly, and most high time engines will fail such a test even though there's nothing really wrong other than a minor valve timing issue. If you do want to go deeper, negotiate with the seller, but understand that the purchaser should pay in full for such tests to be carried out and be liable for any damage caused. If these tests are refused by the seller under all circumstances, it's up to the purchaser to weigh the risk. Rating is for passing one or both tests: full points to null points and walk away.

Evaluation procedure
Add up the total points scored!
150 to 160 points = excellent to almost concours class; hope it doesn't break.
140 to 149 points = good to very good, but it's going to cost to keep it this way.
120 to 139 points = average to good, but where were the problems found?
110 to 119 points = below average to average; careful consideration required.
100 to 109 points = borderline money pit.
80 to 99 points = beware; it's going to cost a lot of money, what's the purchase price?
79 points or less = run away, unless you want to turn a big fortune into a small one.

If any car scores less than 100 from such a detailed inspection, the buyer needs to carefully consider their purchasing position because it's definitely going to be a money pit. Restoration of such a complicated piece of machinery to full roadworthiness is a labour of love, as the money sunk into it cannot be recovered.

Rose-coloured glasses can disguise a multitude of sins, but this puppy is a perfect example; top 1 per cent.

10 Auctions
– sold! Another way to buy your dream

Auction pros & cons

Pros: Prices will usually be lower than those of dealers or private sellers and you might grab a real bargain on the day. Auctioneers have usually established clear title with the seller. At the venue you can usually examine documentation relating to the vehicle.
Cons: You have to rely on a sketchy catalogue description of condition and history. The opportunity to inspect is limited and you cannot drive the car. Auction cars are often a little below par and may require some work. It's easy to overbid. There will usually be a buyer's premium to pay in addition to the auction hammer price.

Which auction?

Auctions by established auctioneers are advertised in car magazines and on the auction houses' websites. A catalogue, or a simple printed list of the lots for auction might only be available a day or two ahead, though often lots are listed and pictured on auctioneers' websites much earlier. Contact the auction company to ask if previous auction selling prices are available, as this is useful information (details of past sales are often available on websites).

Catalogue, entry fee & payment details

When you purchase the catalogue of the vehicles in the auction, it often acts as a ticket allowing two people to attend the viewing days and auction. Catalogue details tend to be comparatively brief, but will include information such as 'one owner from new,' 'low mileage,' 'full service history,' etc. It will also usually show a guide price to give you some idea of what to expect to pay, and will tell you what is charged as a 'buyer's premium.' The catalogue will also contain details of acceptable forms of payment. At the fall of the hammer an immediate deposit is usually required, the balance payable within 24 hours. If the plan is to pay by cash, there may be a cash limit. Some auctions will accept payment by debit card. Sometimes credit or charge cards are acceptable, but will often incur an extra charge. A bank draft or bank transfer will have to be arranged in advance with your own bank as well as with the auction house. No car will be released before all payments are cleared. If delays occur in payment transfers then storage costs can accrue.

Buyer's premium

A buyer's premium will be added to the hammer price: don't forget this in your calculations. It is not usual for there to be a further state tax or local tax on the purchase price and/or on the buyer's premium.

Viewing

In some instances it's possible to view on the day, or days before, as well as in the hours prior to the auction. There are auction officials available who are willing to help out by opening engine and luggage compartments and to allow you to inspect the interior. While the officials may start the engine for you, a test drive is out of the question. Crawling under and around the car as much as you want is permitted, but you can't suggest that the car you are interested in be jacked up, or attempt to do the job yourself. You can also ask to see any documentation available.

Bidding

Before you take part in the auction, decide your maximum bid – and stick to it!

It may take a while for the auctioneer to reach the lot you are interested in, so use that time to observe how other bidders behave. When it's the turn of your car, attract the auctioneer's attention and make an early bid. The auctioneer will then look to you for a reaction every time another bid is made; usually the bids will be in fixed increments until the bidding slows, when smaller increments will often be accepted before the hammer falls. If you want to withdraw from the bidding, make sure the auctioneer understands your intentions – a vigorous shake of the head when he or she looks to you for the next bid should do the trick!

Assuming that you are the successful bidder, the auctioneer will note your card or paddle number, and from that moment on you will be responsible for the vehicle.

If the car is unsold, either because it failed to reach the reserve or because there was little interest, it may be possible to negotiate with the owner, via the auctioneers, once the sale is over.

Successful bid

There are two more items to think about. How to get the car home, and insurance? If you can't drive the car, your own or a hired trailer is one way, another is to have the vehicle shipped using the facilities of a local company. The auction house will also have details of companies specialising in the transfer of cars.

Insurance for immediate cover can usually be purchased on site, but it may be more cost-effective to make arrangements with your own insurance company in advance, and then call to confirm the full details.

eBay & other online auctions

eBay & other online auctions could land you a Turbo at a bargain price, though you'd be foolhardy to bid without examining the car first; something most vendors encourage. A useful feature of eBay is that the geographical location of the car is shown, so you can narrow your choices to those within a realistic radius of home. Be prepared to be outbid in the last few moments of the auction. Remember, your bid is binding and that it will be very, very difficult to get restitution in the case of a crooked vendor fleecing you – caveat emptor!

Be aware that some cars offered for sale in online auctions are 'ghost' cars. Don't part with any cash without being sure that the vehicle does actually exist and is as described (usually pre-bidding inspection is possible).

Auctioneers

Barrett-Jackson www.barrett-jackson.com/
Bonhams www.bonhams.com/
British Car Auctions BCA) www.bca-europe.com or www.british-car-auctions.co.uk/
Cheffins www.cheffins.co.uk/
Christies www.christies.com/

Copart www.copart.com/
Coys www.coys.co.uk/
ebay www.ebay.com/
H&H www.classic-auctions.co.uk/
RM www.rmauctions.com/
Shannons www.shannons.com.au/
Silver www.silverauctions.com

11 Paperwork
– correct documentation is essential!

The paper trail

Over the years the Porsche 930 or 911 (930) Turbo should have accumulated a large portfolio of paperwork representing its real history. From it can be deduced the level of care the car has received, which specialists have worked on it and the dates of major repairs and restorations. This information is priceless to you, the new owner. Be wary of cars with little paperwork to support their claimed history. The correct owner's manual is also vitally important, so check the glove compartment for it.

Registration documents

All countries/states have some form of registration for private vehicles whether it's like the American 'pink slip' system, German TÜV, Swiss MFK or the British 'log book' systems. It's essential to check the registration document is genuine, that it relates to the car in question and that all of its details are correctly recorded, including chassis/VIN and engine numbers. The previous owner's name and address will be recorded in the documentation when purchasing direct; this will not be the case with dealers.

In the UK the current (Euro-aligned) registration document is named 'V5C,' and is printed in coloured sections of blue, green and pink. The blue section relates to the car specification, the green section has details of the new owner, and the pink section is sent to the DVLA in the UK when the car is sold. A small section in yellow deals with selling the car within the motor trade.

In the UK the DVLA will provide details of earlier keepers of the vehicle upon payment of a small fee and much can be learned in this way.

If the car has a foreign registration, there may be expensive and time-consuming formalities to complete – do you really want the hassle?

Roadworthiness certificate

Most administrations require that vehicles are regularly tested to prove they are safe to use on public highways and do not produce excessive emissions. In the UK that test (the 'MoT') is carried out at approved testing stations, for a fee. In American states requirements vary dramatically. In Switzerland and Germany roadworthy and emissions tests are mandatory.

If the car looks unusual, only the paperwork can provide the necessary provenance. (Author's collection)

In the UK the test is required on an annual basis once a vehicle becomes three years old. Of particular relevance for older cars is that the certificate issued includes the mileage reading recorded at the test date and, therefore, becomes an independent record of that car's history. Ask the seller if previous certificates are available. Without a MoT the vehicle should be taken on a flat-bed to its new home, unless you insist that a valid MoT is part of the deal, which is best because it's another inspection and another set of eyes.

Road licence

Administrations around the world charge some kind of tax for the use of its road system. The actual form of the 'road licence' and how it is displayed varies.

Whatever the form of the 'road licence,' it must relate to the vehicle carrying it and be present and valid if the car is to be driven on the public highway legally. The value of the license will depend on the length of time it will continue to be valid.

In the UK if a car is untaxed because it has not been used for a period of time, the owner has to inform the licensing authorities, otherwise the vehicle's date-related registration number will be lost and there will be a painful amount of paperwork to get it re-registered. Also in the UK, vehicles built before the end of 1972 are provided with 'tax discs' free of charge (which must be valid and on display). Car clubs can often provide formal proof that a particular car qualifies for this valuable concession.

Certificates of authenticity
For 911 (930) Turbo models manufactured from model year 1982 it's possible to obtain a certificate of authenticity from your local Porsche dealer, however, be aware that this documentation is accompanied by a hefty fee and accuracy is suspect. If the car was manufactured before model year 1982, obtaining original factory records from the factory is far more difficult, but possible.

If the car has been used in European classic car rallies, it may have a FIVA (Federation Internationale des Vehicules Anciens) certificate. The so-called 'FIVA Passport,' or 'FIVA Vehicle Identity Card,' enables organisers and participants to recognise whether or not a particular vehicle is suitable for individual events. If you want to obtain such a certificate go to www.fbhvc.co.uk or www.fiva.org (there will be similar organisations in other countries, too).

Valuation certificate
Hopefully, the seller will have a recent valuation certificate, or letter signed by a recognised expert stating how much he, or she, believes the particular car to be worth (such documents, together with photos, are usually needed to get 'agreed value' insurance). Generally, such documents should act only as confirmation of your own assessment of the car rather than a guarantee of value, as the expert has probably not seen the car in the flesh. The easiest way to find out how to obtain a formal valuation is to contact the owners' club.

Service history
Many 930 and 911 (930) Turbo models will have been serviced at home by enthusiastic and hopefully, capable owners. Nevertheless, try to obtain as much service history and other paperwork pertaining to the car as you can. Genuine dealer stamps and/or specialist garage receipts score most points in the value stakes. However, anything helps in the great authenticity game, items like the original bill of sale, owner's manual, parts invoices and repair bills adding to the story and character of the car. If the seller claims that the car has been restored, expect receipts and other evidence from a specialist restorer.

If the seller claims to have carried out regular servicing, ask what work was completed, when, and seek some evidence of it being carried out. Your assessment of the car's overall condition should tell you whether the seller's claims are genuine.

Restoration photographs
If the seller tells you that the car has been fully or partially restored, expect to be shown a series of photographs taken while the restoration was under way.

12 What's it worth?
– let your head rule your heart

Heart & head
I always believe you will 'know' the Porsche that's right for you. It's the one that puts a permanent smile on your face, and causes your heart to race like the first time you were in love. However, this is a cruel world, and you must not let your heart rule your head. If you get it wrong, your heart will sink, and that may just be the start of your troubles.

Condition
If the car you've been looking at is really bad, you've probably not bothered to use the marking system in chapter 9. You may not have even got as far as using that chapter at all! If you did use the marking system, you'll know whether the car is in Excellent (maybe Concours), Good, Average or Poor condition or, perhaps, somewhere in-between these categories.

Many car magazines run a regular price guide. If you haven't bought the latest editions, do so now and compare their suggested values for the model you are thinking of buying. Also check the auction prices they're reporting. Values have been fairly stable for some time, but some models will always be more sought-after than others. Trends can change, too. The values published tend to vary from one magazine to another, as do scales of condition, so read carefully the guidance notes provided. Bear in mind that a car that is truly a recent show winner could be worth more than the highest scale published. If the car you have in mind is not in show/ concours condition, relate the level of condition that you judge the car to be in with the appropriate guide price. How does the figure compare with the asking price? Before you start haggling with the seller, consider what affect any variation from standard specification might have on the car's value. If you are buying from a dealer, remember there will be a dealer's premium (profit margin) on the price.

Desirable options/extras
All-leather interior
Original sports seats
Factory-painted body-colour wheels

Undesirable features
Repainted and/or the original colour changed
Modified engine
Noisy aftermarket exhaust modifications
Modern wheels

Warranty
Commercial car dealers have to provide a minimum period of warranty on certain items on any car, but in the real world is the warranty worth the paper it's written on? Look around; is the dealer capable of repairing a Porsche? What's covered by the warranty? How far from the dealer do you live? How are you going to get the car back to the dealer? What about purchasing extended warranty policies? Ask yourself the same questions. Is the company underwriting the warranty policy going

to be around in two years? Warranty, unless purchasing from a reputable approved Porsche dealer, should not be a purchase consideration, as nine times out of ten when something fails it is not going to be repaired under any warranty scheme without a fight, and more often than not the buyer loses. Maybe it might be worth getting a discount on the purchase price and foregoing the warranty altogether?

Private purchases are not protected by mandatory warranty requirements, and getting a previous owner to pay for undisclosed problems and any repairs usually involves legal action.

Pre-purchase inspection (PPI)
This buyer's guide contains many procedures that you as the buyer can follow, but I still strongly recommend that any Porsche being seriously considered for purchase be taken to a recognised expert; usually a dealer for a fully independent inspection. A PPI should also detect any legal issues such as forged registration papers, which are becoming an ever increasing problem in the UK after the theft of hundreds of thousands of official V5 forms in 2006. Ringing of VINs or detecting clones of legally registered cars does require expertise, but nothing is ever guaranteed. You will have to pay for such an inspection but it's worth it.

Striking a deal
Negotiate on the basis of your condition assessment, mileage, and fault rectification cost. Also take into account the car's specification. Be realistic about the value, but don't be completely intractable; a small compromise on the part of the vendor or buyer will often facilitate a deal at little real cost. However, it's critical that you use your evaluation points score as your basis for negotiating the price down. If you have identified problems you know are going to cost a lot of money to rectify, you must insist these costs be deducted from the final purchase price. It's far better to walk away from a deal than to let your heart rule your head – there is always a better deal out there somewhere.

13 Do you really want to restore?
– it'll take longer and cost more than you think

The Porsche 930 or 911 (930) Turbo is not a normal 'car,' and does not have the more traditional separate chassis and body assembly. Its unibody or monocoque construction is an extremely complicated piece of design and engineering, and very difficult to pull part, repair and put back together properly. The biggest issue with structural repair of the unibody is firstly getting all the right parts, then jigging and clamping them correctly into position before welding accurately, and treating the metalwork (including the weld joints to ensure that rust cannot form in and around the repair during the restoration and after it's been painted).

Specialist tools and equipment, including a proper assembly jig, are required for all structural repairs, as is the factory workshop structural repair manual, which must be followed to the letter. There are no short cuts when the objective is to repair the structure properly.

In summary, the Porsche Turbo model range are all pieces of precision engineering not easily restored, but if you are not convinced, read on.

Questions & answers

● The biggest cost in any restoration is labour. Can you do it all yourself or do you need professional help?
● How are your welding and painting skills?
● Do you have the required tooling and specialist equipment (including a monocoque jig) for any structural repairs?
● Do you have the Porsche workshop structural repair manual?
● Do you have the facilities?
● Do you have an approved Porsche dealer nearby?
● Do you have the time?
● What are your time expectations for the job? Your dedication is strong now, but will it still be in two years' time?

This model year 1979 911 (930) Turbo rolling chassis was offered for sale in the US for ●x4375 ... (Author's collection)

... ditto ... (Author's collection)

... are you up for the job? ... (Author's collection)

... you'll need an engine ... (Courtesy Tobias Aschbacher)

• If you cannot do the work yourself, can you afford professional restoration? A full external and internal restoration (including engine and transmission rebuilds) is going to cost a huge amount in any currency.
• Is a rolling chassis restoration an option?
• In theory if a full 'nut-and-bolt' restoration is intended, it's usually best to buy the worst car you can find (so long as certain components are good), but how will you know what's good and what's not without specialist test equipment and knowledge?
• Will the money ploughed into a full restoration ever be recovered? Not a chance. In the Porsche world originality is always worth more than restored. A Porsche restoration can only be approached as a labour of love as it makes no economic sense.

... all the right equipment ...
(Courtesy Tobias Aschbacher)

... and Tobias' skill level. Still up for the job?
(Courtesy Tobias Aschbacher)

14 Paint problems
– bad complexion, including dimples, pimples and bubbles

Paint faults generally occur due to lack of protection and/or maintenance, or poor preparation prior to a repaint or touch-up. Some of the following conditions may be present in the car you're looking at:

Orange peel (bad)
Most Porsches leave the factory with a slight orange peel look. However, bad orange peel is an uneven paint surface, similar to the appearance of the skin of an orange. The fault is caused by the failure of atomized paint droplets to flow into each other when they hit the surface. It's sometimes possible to rub out the effect with proprietary paint cutting/rubbing compound or very fine grades of abrasive paper. A repaint may be necessary in severe cases. Consult a bodywork repairer/paint shop for advice on the particular car.

Cracking
Severe cases are likely to have been caused by too heavy an application of paint (or filler beneath the paint). Insufficient stirring of the paint before application can lead to the components being improperly mixed, also resulting in cracking. Incompatibility with the paint already on the panel can have a similar effect, too. To rectify the problem it is necessary to rub down to a smooth, sound finish before repainting the problem area. Rolling of fenders (guards or wings) can cause cracking.

Crazing
Sometimes the paint takes on a crazed rather than a cracked appearance when the problems mentioned under 'Cracking' are present. This problem can also be caused by a reaction between the underlying surface and the paint. Paint removal and repainting the problem area is usually the only solution.

From model year 1976 all Turbo model body styles were subjected to a galvanisation protection process. (Courtesy Porsche AG archive)

Standard Porsche paint; slight orange peel look. (Courtesy Porsche AG archive)

Solid paint colours oxidise when exposed to sunlight for long periods of time. (Courtesy Porsche AG archive)

Blistering

On the 930 and 911 (930) Turbo model range blistering it's always caused by rust developing underneath the paint. Usually perforation will be found in the metal and the damage will be worse than that suggested by the area of blistering. The metal will have to be repaired before repainting.

Wheels painted in the body colour are normal and withstand the ravages of time well. (Courtesy Porsche AG archive)

Micro blistering

Often the result of economic repaints. Consult a paint specialist, but usually damaged paint will have to be removed before a partial or full repaint.

Fading & oxidation

Some colours, especially solid reds, are prone to fading and oxidation if subjected to strong sunlight for long periods without polish protection. Sometimes proprietary paint restorers and/or paint cutting/rubbing compounds will retrieve the situation. Often a repaint is the only real solution.

Is this the original paint? (Author's collection)

Peeling

Often a problem with metallic paintwork begins when the sealing lacquer becomes damaged and begins to peel off. Poorly applied paint may also peel. The remedy is to strip and start again!

Dimples

Dimples in the paintwork are caused by the residue of polish (particularly silicone types) not being removed properly before repainting. Paint removal and repainting is the only solution.

There's some work for Dentmaster on this car! (Author's collection)

Dents

Small dents are usually easily cured by the 'Dentmaster,' or equivalent process, that sucks or pushes out the dent (as long as the paint surface is still intact). Companies offering dent removal services usually come to your home: consult your telephone directory.

15 Problems due to lack of use
– just like their owners, Porsche 930/911 (930) Turbos need exercise!

Internal corrosion

The 930 and 911 (930) Turbo models are all fitted with a dry sump horizontally opposed six-cylinder engine, meaning that most of the oil is stored in an external oil tank (located behind the right rear wheel) when the engine is switched off. The only protection against the onset of corrosion once the engine is stationary is the oil film left on the engine's components. If the engine remains stationary for a period of time, gravity takes over and this oil drains away, down into the heads, leaving areas of bare metal unprotected. Over a long period of lack of use corrosion will start on any unprotected, exposed areas of metal, but that's not all, there's another problem. Oil starts to break down (separates into various chemical compounds). Depending on the type of oil (mineral or synthetic) some of the chemical compounds will recombine, forming an acidic residue that corrodes any exposed metal it comes in contact with. Modern petrol blends with an ethanol content of more than 10 per cent will also cause internal corrosion of the fuel delivery system right up to the fuel injectors. Corroded fuel manifold lines can result in a fuel leak and fire when the engine starts.

Seized components

Pistons in brake callipers will seize due to corrosion, as the dust caps and seals dry out, crack and fail.

Moisture in the brake fluid used in the brake system, and from model year 1989 in the hydraulic clutch activation system, will start internal corrosion in the metal pipes.

The main components affected are:
• Brake master cylinder.
• Clutch master and slave cylinders (from model year 1989).
• Brake pads may stick to the brake discs (rotors).
• Brake discs (rotors) will rust.
• The clutch may seize if the clutch plate becomes stuck to the flywheel because of corrosion.
• The handbrake (emergency or parking) will seize as cables and linkages rust. The handbrake assembly is installed in the rear wheel hubs (brake-shoe system) and is quite complicated, and yes, expensive to repair if it seizes.

Lack of use often leads to the onset of rust ... (Author's collection)

Internal seals

Without fluid for lubrication even synthetic rubber seals will start to dry out and break down. The 3- and 3.3-litre turbocharged engines use a large number of O-rings and gaskets. Long-term storage with due care and attention will result in many oil leaks once it's started again. The same issue applies to the braking system.

External seals

As time passes body panel, luggage compartment lid, door, window and roof system seals used to protect the car against water ingress will harden, crack and fail.

Fluids
• Old acidic oil will corrode any exposed metal it can get to.
• Brake fluid absorbs water from the atmosphere and must be renewed every two years.
• Untreated water left in the windscreen (windshield) washer system will stagnate.

... and in the worst case scenario a lot of restoration work is required. (Courtesy Porsche AG archive)

Tyres & wheels
Tyres that have had the weight of the car on them in a single position for some time will develop flat spots, resulting in driving vibrations. The tyre walls may develop cracks or (blister-type) bulges, and aged rubber can become too hard and unsafe.

Corroded wheels are expensive to repair and/or replace.

Self-levelling, hydro-pneumatic suspension (MacPherson) struts & dampers
With lack of use struts and dampers seals will fail, allowing the gas that forms part of the internal damping system to escape, and eventually collapse.

Rubber
Rubber hoses are used throughout the car, which can harden and crack. This causes all sorts of problems, including fuel leaks, which can lead to a serious engine bay fire.

Electrics
Leaving a battery installed without driving and/ or another form of trickle charging will result in it going completely flat in less than four weeks. In winter it will go flat even faster. If a lead acid battery is left discharged for long periods of time, it will fail completely and will have to be replaced.

Moisture and mould can destroy the most beautiful of interiors. (Courtesy Porsche AG archive)

Earth/grounding problems, especially in the engine bay, are common, and the negative (ground) battery cable is known to corrode internally. Sparkplugs will corrode, lead insulation hardens and cracks, and all exposed electrical wiring looms may be targeted by rodents looking for food and a new home.

Rotting exhaust system
Exhaust gas always contains some water, and if it sits for long periods of time in a cold exhaust system, it will cause the system to rot from the inside. The outside of the exhaust system will also rust over time.

Mould
Any moisture inside the car with the right environmental conditions will result in mould spreading throughout the entire interior.

16 The Community

– key people, organisations and companies in the Porsche world

This chapter provides various sources that a prospective 930 or 911 (930) Turbo owner can seek advice and guidance from. The entire turbocharged model range has a huge and enthusiastic following around the world.

Books

Porsche 911 Story by Paul Frère, published by Patrick Stephens Limited.
ISBN: 0-85059-175-9

Original Porsche 911 by Peter Morgan, published by Bay View Books.
ISBN: 1-901432-16-5 and 978-1-901432-16-9

Porsche 911 Red Book 1965-1999 by Patrick C. Paternie, published by MBI Publishing Company.
ISBN: 0-7603-0723-7 and 978-0-760307-23-6

Porsche Typenatlas Serienfahrzeuge by Marc Bongers, published by BECHTERMÜNZ VERLAG.
ISBN: 3-8289-5354-9 and 978-3-828953-54-3

Magazines

Occasionally, a 930 or 911 (930) Turbo article appears in a 21st century edition of a Porsche or car related magazine. There were however, many magazines published in the 1970s, 80s and 90s filled with reviews and stories on the entire model range; *Excellence* in the USA is a prime example.

Porsche maintenance services

Autofarm (1973) Ltd
Oddington Grange
Weston-on-the-Green
Oxfordshire
OX25 3QW
England
Tel: +44 (0)1865 331234
www.autofarm.co.uk

Porsch-Apart Ltd
Unit 4 Field Mill
Harrison Street
Ramsbottom
Bury
Lancashire
BL0 0AH
England
Tel: +44 (0) 1706 824053
www.porsch-apart.co.uk

Berlyn Services
9 Fore Street
Ilfracombe
EX34 9ED
England
Tel: +44 (0)1271 866818

www.partsforporsche.co.uk
RAC Performance
Parent company of RUF Auto Centre
3219 Commander Drive
Dallas
TX 75006
USA
Tel: +1 214 269 1570 or 1-888-783-6872
www.racperformance.com

Porsche clubs
The author has been involved with some UK and European based Porsche clubs in the past and is happy to recommend:

http://www.porscheclubgb.com/
Porsche Club Great Britain Registered office
Cornbury House
Cotswold Business Village, London Road
Moreton-in-Marsh
Gloucestershire
GL56 0JQ
England
Tel: +44 (0)1608 652911

http://www.tipec.net/ (The Independent Porsche Enthusiasts Club)
TIPEC Club Office
10 Whitecroft Gardens
Woodford Halse
Northants
NN11 3PY
England
Tel: +44 (0) 8456 020052

Internet based Porsche communities
North American readers please check with the Porsche Club America website (www.pca.org) to find the contact address of the PCA region nearest to you.

Google is your friend. There are many internet based Porsche communities in almost every country in the world. Use the search words Porsche, 911, 930 or Turbo to get started, or check out:
http://porsche930turbo.com/
http://www.type930.com/
@porscheturbo930 on Twitter

17 Vital statistics
– essential data at your fingertips

Production numbers

Total 930 & 911 (930) Turbo model production from model year 1975 to 1989			
Model year	Number produced	Model year	Number produced
1975	284	1983	1080
1976	1174	1984	881
1977	1422	1985	1148
1978	1257	1986	2670
1979	2052	1987	3094*
1980	840	1988	2784**
1981	761	1989	2743***
1982	1027	–	–

*Includes 200 production line slant-nose versions
**Includes 296 production line slant-nose versions
***Includes 180 production line slant-nose versions

RoW market engine specifications

Engine type	930.50/52	930.60*	930.66*
Bore mm (in)	95 (3.74)	97 (3.82)	
Stroke mm (in)	70.4 (2.77)	74.4 (2.93)	
Displacement cc (cu.in)	2994 (182.7)	3299 (201.3)	
Compression ratio	6.5:1	7.0:1	
Horsepower (kw/hp)@rpm	191/260@5500	221/300@5500	221/300@5500
Torque (Nm/ft-lb)@rpm	343/253@4000	412/304@4000	430/317@4000
Maximum rpm	6000		
Original fuel octane	98 RON leaded		
Oil pressure at 5000 rpm (oil temperature 80°C/176°F)	4.5 bar (65psi)		
Oil consumption	Approximately 1.5 litres per 1000km (1.6USqt per 621 miles)		

*From model year 1983 an engine enhancement (power upgrade) kit was available from Porsche Exclusive boosting engine output to 243Kw (330hp) at 5750rpm and an increase in torque to 467Nm (344ft-lb) at 4500rpm

US & Japan market engine specifications

Engine type	930.51/53/54	930.61/62/63/64/65	930.68
Bore mm (in)	95 (3.74)	97 (3.82)	
Stroke mm (in)	70.4 (2.77)	74.4 (2.93)	
Displacement cc (cu.in)	2994 (182.7)	3299 (201.3)	
Compression ratio	6.5:1	7.0:1	
Horsepower (Kw/hp)@rpm	180/245@5500	195/265@5500	207/282@5000
Torque (Nm/ft-lb)@rpm	343/253@4000	395/291@4000	389/287@4000
Maximum rpm	6000		
Fuel octane	98 RON leaded	91 to 96 RON unleaded	
Oil pressure at 5000 rpm (oil temperature 90°C/194°F)	4.5 bar (65psi)		
Oil consumption	Approximately 1.5 litres per 1000km (1.6USqt per 621 miles)		

Transmission types

Type	Model year(s)	Comments
930.30	1975	Four-speed manual for all models/markets
930.32	1976	Four-speed manual for models fitted with 50 profile tyres
930.33	1977	Four-speed manual for all models/markets
930.34	1978 to 1985	Four-speed manual for all models/markets
930.36	1986 to 1988	Four-speed manual for all models/markets
G50.50	1989	Five-speed manual courtesy of Alois Ruf and Getrag for all models/markets

All four-speed 930 and the five-speed G50.50 transmission fitted to the 930 and 911 (930) Turbo model range were offered with an optional limited slip differential (LSD). Some special edition models, such as the 911 Turbo Sport, were delivered to customers with LSD installed as part of the 'sport' package.

Basic brake system specifications

Model (model years)	Boost system	Front & rear callipers	Front & rear discs (rotors)
930 Coupé (1975 to 1977)	None	2-piston	Vented/solid
911 (930) Coupé (1978 & 1979)	Vacuum servo	2-piston	Vented/solid
911 (930) Coupé (1980 to 1986)	Vacuum servo	4-piston	Vented/perforated
911 (930) Coupé, Targa & Cabriolet (1987 to 1989)	Vacuum servo	4-piston	Vented/perforated

Basic model dimensions

Model	Length mm (in)	Width mm (in)	Roof height* mm (in)
930 Coupé	4291 (169)	1775 (70)	1320 (52)
911 (930) Coupé classic & slant-nose	4291 (169)	1775 (70)	1310 (51.5)
911 (930) Targa classic & slant-nose	4291 (169)	1775 (70)	1310 (51.5)
911 (930) Cabriolet classic & slant-nose	4291 (169)	1775 (70)	1320 (51.5)

Basic model empty weights

Model & year/s	Weight kg (lb)
930 Coupé 1975	1140 (2513)
930 Coupé 1976 & 1977	1195 (2635)
911 (930) Coupé 1978 to 1985	1300 (2866)
911 (930) Coupé 1986 to 1989	1335 (2943)
911 (930) slant-nose Coupé Sport SE 1983 to 1985	1300 (2866) (2943)
911 (930) slant-nose Coupé Sport SE 1986 to 1989	1335 (2943)
911 (930) Targa	1335 (2943)
911 (930) Cabriolet	1335 (2943)

Add 90kg (198.4lbs) to basic weight for all official US market versions.

Approved tyres

Porsche approved & tested summer tyres for complete 930 & 911 (930) Turbo model range
Manufacturer & model, dimensions, N-rating, (wheel size)
Pirelli P Zero Directional, 205/55 ZR16, N3, (7Jx16)
Bridgestone Potenza S-02, 205/55 ZR16, N3, (7Jx16)
Continental ContiSportContact, 205/55 ZR16, N2, (7Jx16)
Michelin SX MXX3, 205/55 ZR16, N2, (7Jx16)
Pirelli P Zero Directional, 225/50 ZR16, N3, (8Jx16)
Bridgestone Potenza S-02, 225/50 ZR16, N3, (8Jx16)
Continental ContiSportContact, 225/50 ZR16, N2, (8Jx16)
Michelin SX MXX3, 225/50 ZR16, N2, (8Jx16)
Continental ContiSportContact, 245/45 ZR16, N1, (9Jx16)
Michelin SX MXX3, 245/45 ZR16, N2, (9Jx16)

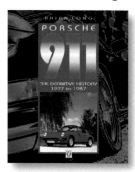
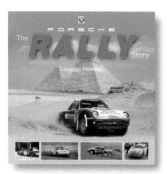
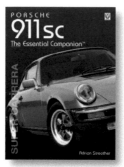
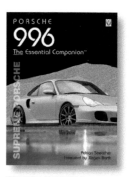